Secrets to Starting & Running Your Own Bookkeeping Business:
Freelance Bookkeeping At Home
By Sylvia Jaumann

Starting a bookkeeping business is one of the least expensive home-based businesses to begin. However, you may have a lot of questions about how to set up your bookkeeping business such as, "How do I find clients?" Or, "How do I keep track of all my clients' paperwork?" Or, "How much should I charge per hour?"

As long as you are a competent bookkeeper with several years of experience, you will be able to open your bookkeeping business very quickly with the help of this guide.

"I was impressed with the amount of information regarding organization—I consider myself organized, but there were a number of great hints for putting together customer files and developing binders that I hadn't considered."

Ed Mueller
Asset Bookkeeping Service

"I love the book due to the fact that it answered a lot of questions and concerns that I had in regards to starting and setting up my bookkeeping business. I now have a better understanding of how to become organized and how to promote and market my business."

Charlene S. Bey
All Bey Bookkeeping, LLC

"Your book was very instrumental and provided excellent guidance! By following your steps, I had my home office ready, so when I got my first client, everything was already set up."

Robin L. Brown
Daybreak Bookkeeping

Editor: Cynthia Sherwood

This publication is designed to provide accurate and
authoritative information in regard to the subject matter
covered. It is sold the understanding that the publisher is not
engaged in rendering legal, accounting, or other professional
services. If legal advice or other expert assistance is required, the
services of a competent professional person should be sought.

ISBN: 0973887923
EAN-13: 978-0973887921

Printed in the United States of America

Dedication

This book is dedicated to my parents Norm and Rose, who showed me how running your own business is the best way to go and without whom my fascination with numbers and calculators would not exist; my sister Nicole, who has always been my rock and supported everything I did; and my son Cody, who has inspired me to succeed in so many ways.

Table of Contents

*Small opportunities are often the beginning
of great enterprises.*
Demosthenes (384 BC - 322 BC)

Introduction

The demand for good bookkeepers is at an all time high as more people make the leap into self-employment each year and need competent bookkeeping help.

These entrepreneurs are searching for their slice of the pie by starting their own successful business ventures. This leaves the door wide open for a talented bookkeeper such as you to cash in on this trend by helping these businesses with their finances.

Don't let anybody tell you that now is not a good time to start a bookkeeping business because of the economy. Yes, the economy is in rough shape and many people are experiencing layoffs. No one is disputing that these are tough times.

But this volatile economy is forcing many people to take action with their financial future. Countless people are looking at their lives and realizing that they need to make drastic changes in order to survive.

For some people, this may mean taking a second job. But for others, who are tired of working for "the man," this means finally starting that business that they've always dreamed of.

These entrepreneurs are starting their businesses using skills they have developed, whether that means plumbing, taking care of children, painting, or any other ability. These business owners all have one common goal: *to successfully start and run their own business.*

What they almost always don't have, however, is the know-how to take care of their own bookkeeping, which is where *you* come in. In general, most business owners *hate* doing their own books.

As an experienced bookkeeper you know that bookkeeping is one of the most challenging, rewarding, and necessary functions of operating a business. If "the books" are not in order, a company can quickly go out of business. Keeping track of revenues and expenses is the key to a successful business.

Your reasons for wanting to start a bookkeeping business will probably be as individual as you are. Maybe you're a mother who wants to stay home with her children and still earn a decent living. Or maybe you're a bookkeeper who has worked in the corporate world for many years and are ready to take on the challenge of running your own bookkeeping practice.

Whatever your personal reasons, you have come to the right source for information on starting your bookkeeping business. You have many questions, and my goal for this book is to provide the answers so you can quickly get started in this in-demand field.

You will need to have several years of hands-on bookkeeping experience under your belt before you even consider starting your own bookkeeping business. You should also have above-average bookkeeping skills.

You may want to consider working for an accounting firm or established bookkeeping business prior to launching your own practice. This in itself will provide you with very useful training and knowledge.

It's also important to get a range of bookkeeping experience by working for all levels of businesses: proprietorship, partnership and corporate. Make an effort to do bookkeeping for as many different types of businesses as you can, such as service, retail and non-profit.

You should also have some business and time management skills, although this book will guide you through the basics.

Here are some skills you should either have or be able to acquire:

- Good social skills to deal with clients and other business professionals

- Self-motivation to handle your own schedule

- Ability to plan a marketing strategy

- Self-confidence and ability to overcome shyness to promote your business

- Capability of planning strategies to overcome challenges when they arise

- Persistence to not give up when the going gets tough

- Excellent organizational skills to be able to juggle multiple clients at once

As a bookkeeper you will never stop learning, which really is the *best* part of this business. It never gets boring and you're always discovering new information.

This book is written with the assumption that you have the experience required to operate a bookkeeping business and are just searching for the right systems and procedures to set up your business.

The information in this book can be applied to any country and is not specific to any one location. Although it was written in Canada, the information is applicable wherever you are.

If you're already an established freelance bookkeeper, you don't have to read this book from front to back. You can jump around and read the chapters that apply to you first, so you can get started right away. However, I highly recommend that you come back and read the entire book when you have the time to truly benefit from all the tips that are packed into this book. So let's get started!

Chapter I: Getting Started

Success in business requires training and discipline and hard work. But if you're not frightened by these things, the opportunities are just as great today as they ever were.
David Rockefeller, Sr.

Personality Traits You Need to Have

Do you find yourself wondering if you have what it takes to run a home-based bookkeeping business? Not everyone is able to work on his or her own and make a go of it. So, here are five personality traits you must have before you even think about starting your home-based bookkeeping business.

1. Self-Motivation

If you're the kind of person who needs to be told what to do, you'll find running a home-based business very challenging.

Being self-motivated means that you get up every morning and go to your home office just the same way you would if you were an employee.

Routines can help a great deal with self-motivation. Doing things like getting up at the same time every day; going into your office and turning on the lights, computer, and radio; even getting yourself ready as if you're going to work can all put you in the right frame of mind to begin your day.

2. Organization

With all the paperwork you'll be handling for your clients, being organized is critical to your business success. So if you find that paperwork gets scattered all over your desk or if you misplace things a lot, you'll definitely have to improve in this area.

Client paperwork obviously can <u>never</u> be mixed together, so proper handling and filing of each client's information cannot be overstated. Keep your desk clear and only have one set of client files out at a time. When you're done with them, file them away immediately.

3. Ability to Schedule and Plan

As a bookkeeper, you're probably very aware of the importance of deadlines. Clients depend on you to know exactly when a remittance payment is due. If you don't keep track of these important dates, you will lose clients, plain and simple.

A Day-Timer is a great tool for scheduling and planning out your work week. Always write down an upcoming deadline the moment you're aware of it. It's too easy to forget when you're dealing with multiple clients.

4. Persistence

Building a home-based bookkeeping business doesn't happen overnight. It's not a "get rich quick" business. So you must have patience and persistence to build your business slowly. Some months you may not pick up any new clients and others you may get more than you can handle all at one time.

The important thing is to never give up. If one method of promoting your business isn't working, try something different. Keep your eye on your goals.

5. Self-Promotion

You can't be shy about letting people know about your bookkeeping business. Don't be afraid to talk to everybody you come in contact with and let them know about your services.

If you don't want to ask somebody directly if they need a bookkeeper, ask them if they know anyone who needs one (this takes the pressure off and doesn't put the person "on the spot.") Word of mouth is the key to this business, so you have to be able to put yourself out there.

Many people are not born with these five personality traits. But they are skills that can be learned if you have the determination and drive to succeed in your bookkeeping business.

Certification

The one question I get asked the most by visitors to my website is "What type of certification is required to start a bookkeeping business?" My answer has always been that you generally don't need certification in order to be successful as a freelance bookkeeper.

I've personally run my own bookkeeping business without one for years and have never encountered a problem with not being certified.

However, I've come to realize that this may not necessarily be true anymore. I've learned that certification can give you certain benefits, such as:

- Potential clients will trust in your skills and knowledge

- You can charge more for your services

- You'll have more self-confidence knowing you have the necessary education

- Clients can verify that you are certified through your professional organization

In general, certification involves taking an exam where you are tested on your knowledge of typical bookkeeping procedures.

There are certifying bodies in the following countries:

Canada:

The Institute of Professional Bookkeepers of Canada (IPBC)
– www.ipbc.ca

United States:

The American Institute of Professional Bookkeepers (AIPB)
– www.aipb.org

Australia:

The Australian Association of Professional Bookkeepers (AAPB)
– www.aapb.org.au

United Kingdom:

The Institute of Certified Bookkeepers (ICB)
–www.bookkeepers.org.uk/

If your country is not listed above, do a Google search using your country name. For example:

"country + bookkeeper association"

Why Start a Bookkeeping Business?

Most small business owners don't have backgrounds in bookkeeping. They need the expertise that only a skilled and qualified bookkeeper can provide. That's where you come in. Not only is starting a bookkeeping business a great home-based business, but here's why it's the ideal one to start part-time:

You Can Transition Into It

Working part-time doing freelance bookkeeping for about twenty hours per week is a good way to start your bookkeeping practice and not risk your current full-time income.

Unlike many business opportunities today, taking the step to a full-time bookkeeping business is usually a smooth transition. First build up your business and then decide if you want to make the leap to full-time.

You Earn More Money

Every day bookkeepers sell their precious skills to their bosses for a paltry hourly rate when they could be earning top dollar running their own bookkeeping business.

Did you know that the average hourly rate for bookkeepers in Canada is only $14.88 per hour and in the United States it's only $15.57?

As a freelance bookkeeper, you can charge from $20 to $75 per hour. Which would you prefer?

It's Not Hard to Find Clients

With very little marketing effort, you can expect to find one or two clients per month who will welcome your services and happily pay for the expertise that you provide to their businesses. For example, a one-man tradesperson business would be happy to find someone like you to keep his books for him. Then he just has to drop off his receipts and invoices, and you take care of the paperwork for him so he can concentrate on his business.

You'll Have More Security

Even though running a bookkeeping business (or any business for that matter) comes with its share of risks, there is also more security than being employed by someone else. This security comes from the knowledge that once your bookkeeping business is established and you have many different clients, you'll never again have to worry about losing your entire income.

Yes, you may lose a client or two along the way, but this will not affect your income like getting fired or being downsized in a regular job will. That's because most small bookkeeping clients will bring in a few hundred dollars per month each, which won't break you if you lose them.

Being an employee for someone and knowing that you're at their mercy because they can decide at any time to terminate your employment is a helpless feeling. There is security in being your own boss and deciding who you want to work with.

Start-up Equipment

A home-based bookkeeping practice can be started on a shoestring budget and built from there. As long as you have a computer with a good accounting software package and a few basic office supplies, you can start a bookkeeping business in any room of your home and add on later as your business grows.

It is important that you have a separate area to create your office space, whether that's a spare bedroom or an area in the basement. This helps to keep your personal and business affairs separate. It also lets clients know that you're treating your business professionally and they don't have to worry about their confidential information being compromised.

You'll most likely want to find a comfortable desk that you can work at, if you don't already have one. Oftentimes you can find great deals on used office furniture online (i.e. eBay or Craigslist) or in a local used office furniture store.

Accounting & Other Software

When it comes to your accounting software, make sure you don't buy a cheap program just to save a few dollars. You'll regret it down the road when it doesn't provide you with the features you need to do your job properly and potentially cause embarrassment with clients.

The three big accounting software packages that are in use at the time of this writing are:

- Simply Accounting
- QuickBooks
- Peachtree Accounting

You should have one of these accounting packages installed on your computer. I've used Simply Accounting for years and prefer it, but every bookkeeper has his or her own preference. I've noticed that Simply Accounting is more popular with

Canadian bookkeepers and QuickBooks seems to be used more by American bookkeepers.

Keep in mind that you may need more than one accounting package as you acquire clients down the road. This is because you'll find that some clients (if they are not start-ups) may already have their data set up on accounting software that you may not be using.

Most accounting software claims to be exportable from one accounting package to another, but be warned that this may not always be the case. I've personally tried these exports and they have not always succeeded. In some cases I was able to export the main account ledgers but the sub-ledgers would not provide me with the necessary details.

If you are not financially ready to buy more accounting software, you can simply take on these types of clients when their new fiscal year begins. That way you just need to set up their accounts using year-end General Ledger and sub-ledger totals.

As for other software, you should also have a spreadsheet (Excel) and word processing program (Word) such as Microsoft Office. You'll need Word for any sales letters and documents you create for your clients. As a bookkeeper, you probably are familiar with how valuable using an Excel spreadsheet is when handling your financial calculations.

As with all software, you must make sure that you have legal (and not borrowed or pirated) copies of all programs. That's not only because it's illegal to run pirated software, but you never know when you may need to reinstall your software if your computer happens to crash. You don't want that to happen in the middle of a busy time like tax season or year-end, when these things invariably occur.

Computer

You'll also need a newer computer with as fast a speed as you can afford. You will find that using an older computer will end up costing you more time than it's worth.

Also, accounting software is typically updated yearly, so you'll need to make sure that your computer is compatible with the latest updates.

If you're planning on working at your clients' locations, you may need a laptop computer. Fortunately, the cost for laptops has come down in recent years and they are quite affordable whether you use them as your main computer or as a secondary one.

Printer

You should be using a good quality laser printer because you'll be printing loads of pages in your bookkeeping business and as they say "time is money." So buy the best quality laser printer that you can afford.

You may want to invest in a printer/fax/copier/scanner combination machine as this solves all your needs in one piece of equipment. These will typically cost a bit more to start.

Also, if it breaks down, you'll be out all of these features until you can fix or replace the machine. However, if you're working in a small office, they are very convenient to use.

Pay attention to printer toner costs before you buy, however, as they can be quite expensive. You may go through a few of them a year depending on your volume of paperwork.

> **HINT:** You'll find that you can get more mileage out of your laser toner cartridge if you take it out of the machine and shake it a few times when the toner starts to run out. Many times I've put off replacing the cartridge for a week or two just by doing this a few times. There is usually much more toner left in the cartridge than you think.

Desktop Calculator

A good quality desktop calculator is a necessary tool for any bookkeeper. You'll need one that prints out onto a tape for when you're adding up a lot of numbers.

Buy a mid-priced model or the best one that you can afford. This is a tool that you'll be using daily and cheaper models tend to not withstand that kind of use.

Fax Machine

You'll need a fax machine if you don't already have one combined with your printer.

If you don't have a separate phone line for your fax and would like to have a dedicated fax number to give to clients, I recommend using an online fax service such as **eFax.com.**

With these online fax services you receive your faxes in your email account in a PDF file that you can print. Or, if you don't want to print the fax, you don't have to, which saves on the cost of paper.

You can fax directly from your computer using online fax services as long as the document is on your computer already. If you need to fax a document that's not on your computer, you'll need a scanner to send it.

> Here's how I use my online fax service:
>
> - I **send** all my faxes through my fax machine (using my home phone line)
> - I **receive** all my faxes through my online fax service and print them off on my printer
> - I have my online fax number imprinted at the top of my faxes on my home fax machine so it looks like it came directly from my online fax number

If you have a very small budget, you may consider buying a thermal fax machine to start as you can pick these up for next to nothing. That way you can just use the thermal fax machine for your sending outgoing faxes while you receive all your faxes by online fax in your email (and print them with your printer).

However, bear in mind that if you want to use your fax for copying documents, thermal paper is very unstable and will fade with time and heat. But if you have another way to photocopy your documents, this may be an inexpensive option.

Telephone

You will definitely need a separate phone number for your bookkeeping business so you'll know when clients are calling and you can answer the phone professionally.

If you can afford it, consider installing a separate line for your business.

However, if your budget is tight, an easy solution to an expensive business line is to set up a "smart ring" service supplied by your local phone company. You get a separate phone number for your smart ring line but it runs on the same line as your home phone.

Then when a business client calls your smart ring number, you'll hear a distinctive ring that lets you know you've got a business call so you can answer the phone accordingly.

This service is generally quite inexpensive; it costs anywhere from $2 to $5 per month depending on your local phone company and the packages they offer.

You should also have voicemail to take messages from clients when you're unavailable or after business hours. You may find that you prefer working undisturbed at certain parts of your day. That way you can return calls when you're not in the middle of adding up a long list of numbers. Then clients won't think you're ignoring them.

Another calling feature that will make you look good for your clients is "Caller ID." That way if you know who is calling, you can grab any necessary paperwork while the phone is ringing and be more prepared when you talk to your client.

A cell phone is a necessity if you're on the road a lot meeting with clients. That way, if you're calling one client from another client's office, the client you're calling doesn't have to know where you are because you are not using their phone. This helps with client confidentiality.

Vehicle

You'll need a vehicle for meeting with clients as well as picking up any supplies. However, this isn't completely necessary as you can arrange to have clients meet with you and drop off paperwork at your home.

Make sure you carefully record all business driving you do in order to write this off at income tax time. To make this easier, you can use one of those pocket-sized vehicle journal books available in any office supply store to record your mileage.

Bank Account

You may wish to use a personal checking account instead of a business checking account when you first start out to save money on bank charges.

As a bookkeeper you're probably very aware of the costs of a business checking account compared to a personal checking account. So take advantage of this knowledge and have your bookkeeping clients write checks to you using your personal name instead of your business name.

Then, deposit these checks into a separate personal checking account that you've opened in your own name. Use this account for your bookkeeping business transactions only and keep your personal transactions completely separate.

TIP: I have access to both my checking accounts online so when I want to pay myself, all I have to do is a quick transfer from one account to the other. My audit trail is clean and that keeps the government off my back.

Eventually you may want to upgrade to a business account, but I can tell you that most clients have no problem with writing checks to you in your personal name. When you're a freelance bookkeeper who works alone, it's not perceived to be a big issue.

Other Equipment

Here are some other pieces of equipment that you'll want to consider as your business grows:

- File Cabinet: will be necessary to store both your clients' and your own financial records but in the beginning any cardboard box will do.

- Document Shredder: starts at around $20 for a low-end model and should be strongly considered in order to protect your clients' financial information instead of throwing confidential papers in the trash.

- Large Screen Monitor: for your computer to relieve eye strain when you're on the computer looking at numbers all day.

- A Comfortable Chair: will save your back, neck, and shoulders from uncomfortable strain.

Insurance

Insurance is something that you must have in place to protect yourself. At the very least you should have insurance to cover replacement costs should you ever lose all your office equipment due to fire or theft.

Make sure you let your insurer know that you are operating a home business so that you can have this coverage added to your insurance. This is something you should not take lightly. You could easily be put out of business if you lose all your equipment, so your income depends on making a smart decision in this regard.

You may also consider purchasing Liability insurance in case a client injures himself or herself while on your property as well as Errors and Omissions insurance in case of any bookkeeping errors that result in your client being audited. Talk to your insurance agent to learn more.

Neighbors

As a courtesy, you may want to talk to your neighbors and let them know you'll be starting a bookkeeping business.

You should find that it's not too much of a problem with your neighbors as the increase in traffic to your home should be minimal. This is because clients tend to drop off their paperwork monthly or bi-weekly.

You also may decide to pick up paperwork from your clients directly, which will avoid additional traffic altogether.

Business Structure

Most freelance bookkeepers start their business as a sole proprietorship because this is typically the easiest business entity type to set up. This means any income you generate will be taxed on your own personal income tax return and your business is not taxed as a separate entity.

If you're looking for more protection of your personal assets, you may consider starting a corporation. Most home-based bookkeepers don't bother with this, however, as the costs to incorporate can be very high.

If you have any concerns about how your bookkeeping business may affect your personal situation, please make sure you discuss this with a lawyer as I cannot offer any legal advice in this area.

Licenses and Permits

Check with your local government office to make sure that you have the necessary licenses and zoning permits. Failure to do so could result in a fine or having your business shut down.

Even if your bookkeeping business is a home-based one, most local governments require you to have a business license. Some restrict home-based businesses by not allowing clients to come to your home to pick up or drop off information.

Make sure that you research this thoroughly so that you can devise an alternate plan for meeting with your clients if your local area does have such restrictions in place.

Naming Your Bookkeeping Business

Choosing a professional business name for your bookkeeping business will be one of the most important decisions you make. You want to choose a name that projects the ideal image of how your business will be perceived. Easier said than done, right?

To show you how important this process is, let me share a story that happened to me.

About ten years ago I made the mistake of choosing a truly bad name for my first bookkeeping business. I called it "Esquire

Business Services" which, at the time, I thought was a great name because I thought the word "Esquire" gave the business a fancy, legal-sounding name.

I thought that this name would project the image of someone who was smart and knew what she was doing. Boy was I wrong!

I found out later that people who called and got my answering machine were confused by my message and thought that they had reached an escort service! I finally realized I had a <u>bad</u> business name when a lawyer, who was a business associate at the time, phoned my answering machine and thought he'd reached an escort service. Even a professional lawyer didn't understand my "clever" name!

I hope I haven't scared you, but I just want you to see that you have to be very careful when naming your business. The cost and the headache of having to change it can completely set your business back (if not utterly destroy it!)

To get you started in this process, begin by thinking of some descriptive words that would best represent your bookkeeping image.

Here are some examples:

- Accurate
- Reliable
- First Rate

You could also use words that are a "play on words" for bookkeeping, such as:

- Capital
- Bottom Line
- Balanced

Your business name should be easily remembered by potential clients and fairly distinctive. Another option is to use your own name for your business name such as "Susan Adams Bookkeeping Services."

Registering Your Business Name

When you have decided upon a name for your bookkeeping business, you will need to register it. How to do this depends on where you live.

In Canada:

You need to select three potential names in order of preference, fill out a form, and send it to the Government Agent's office for your province. Your potential names are searched. Once you receive approval of your business name, you must register it. There are fees for both the name search and name registration. This process may vary from province to province, so check with your local city hall for more information.

In the United States:

You need to fill out and file a Fictitious Business Name Statement, which is typically available online. You'll have to pay the required fees when you file. Then you just need to publish the name of your business in a local newspaper along with the required fees.

Setup a Tax Account

You'll also need to setup a tax account so that you can collect and remit taxes on your sales. I won't go into specifics on setting up a tax account as this varies depending on the province or state you happen to live in.

Also as a bookkeeper, you are very likely familiar with these procedures as they are typically part of your duties. However, if you have any questions, you can usually find out more information by going online.

Chapter 2: Creating Your Business

Real success is finding your lifework in the work that you love.

David McCullough

Choosing Your Target Market

While creating your business, you need to decide what type of bookkeeping clients you want to work with.

You could serve a broader market, but you'll find greater success if you home in on a specific target market. This will allow you to gain as much knowledge in a specific niche and therefore serve your clients more fully.

Some questions to think about when choosing your target market are:

- Would you prefer working with retail businesses?

- Do you want to specialize in a certain niche business such as a tradesperson or nonprofit?

- Do you like bookkeeping for small corporations or proprietorships?

The answers to these questions will depend upon your experience and your willingness to learn as you go.

For instance, you may have experience doing books for small retail businesses but want to expand and do books for a tradesperson as well.

You may be willing to take on a new tradesperson's books if you have some kind of resource or mentor (such as a bookkeeping associate or an accountant) whom you can rely on for assistance when you have a question. So take this into consideration as you decide what types of clients to look for.

Doing books for corporations, partnerships, and proprietorships also require slightly different procedures and being familiar with these procedures is imperative.

Targeting New Businesses

The majority of businesses that are looking for bookkeepers are new businesses, so this is the main area where you should focus your search for clients.

The easiest way to find these new businesses is to look up new businesses licenses that have been issued in your local area. Most cities and counties now have the names and addresses of new business licensees right on their websites, so this makes it very easy to access and download.

If your local government doesn't provide this information online, call them and ask them to mail or email you a copy of this list.

What Makes a Good Client?

A good client to one bookkeeper may be a bad client to another, as everybody has his or her own individual personality. However, a good client does tend to have three certain traits.

1. They consistently pay your bills on time

2. They are not unreasonable in their need to speak with you (i.e. they don't call you at all hours or drop over unannounced)

3. Their paperwork is always somewhat organized (i.e. they are not consistently missing information which causes delays in processing their paperwork)

1. You won't really know how reliable a client will be with paying your invoices until you actually begin to work with them. But here are some red flags to watch out for before you agree to take them on:

    - They have large amounts of overdue bills in their paperwork

    - They are being pressured by the government to have their taxes done because they haven't filed them in a few years

   If either of these situations apply, always make sure you request a retainer before beginning work for this type of client.

2. In order to prevent your clients from calling you during your off-hours, you must be very clear about what hours you're available to them. This mean stating your office hours clearly and telling them that they must always make an appointment before stopping by.

   Make sure you state this both in writing (in your Engagement Letter or contract) and verbally so there is no misunderstanding about this issue.

   Just because you work at home, doesn't mean you shouldn't be extended the same courtesy all other service businesses enjoy.

3. Having disorganized paperwork is not a huge problem as long as your client is willing to pay the extra costs for having them sorted out by you and they are not missing important paperwork.

If you discover huge gaps of missing information that your client can't account for, you'll have to decide whether or not you want to work with the client.

Ultimately, missing information can reflect poorly on you as it seems as if everyone likes to blame the bookkeeper for any irregularities.

Your Bookkeeping Rates

Research Your Pricing

Do some research on pricing by calling around to different bookkeeping businesses to find out what the going bookkeeping hourly rates are in your local area. This is important because you do not want to overprice or underprice your rates; you want to be competitive.

TIP: Don't just assume that because you're making $15 per hour at your current bookkeeping job that you'll just charge this rate to your clients. You must take your overhead costs into consideration (such as office expenses, utilities, travel time, insurance, etc.) If you don't, you'll end up losing money by not factoring in these costs.

You'll discover when you phone around to your local bookkeeping companies that most of these businesses charge well over the average rate they pay their bookkeeping staff so their business can make a profit. You want to make this profit too. You are in business to make money and to create a better life for yourself, so do your homework on this and don't short-change yourself.

Don't forget to call tax preparers and accountants while doing your research as these are your competitors as well. Many of these professionals offer bookkeeping services and you'll notice that the prices can vary greatly.

If you can, make sure you also contact other home bookkeepers to find out what they are charging. Their prices should definitely be taken into consideration. You may notice that some of them don't charge nearly as much as they should.

Offering Flat Monthly Rates

Once you've decided on your hourly rate, you need to decide if you want to offer flat rates for established clients.

The benefits of this are that both you and your client will have an invoice that is the same each month. Your client will be happy because they won't get any unexpected surprises and you'll know exactly how much you'll be making every month from each client.

To begin with, always start off new bookkeeping clients by charging by the hour. Don't ever let new clients try to talk you into quoting a flat fee before you've had a chance to go through their paperwork.

This is because many well-meaning small business owners have no clue what information you require. So either they'll throw absolutely everything at you (including information that you really don't need) or they'll have huge gaps in paperwork that you *really do need*. This results in lots of wasted time spent tracking information down and sorting it all out.

Generally, you'll probably find when a new client comes to you they will be somewhat behind in their paperwork. This can vary from several months to several years.

That's another reason you want to start off your bookkeeping rates by the hour. You want to make sure that you are paid adequately for sorting out their bookkeeping because it can take many hours spaced over several months to get them caught up again.

Now, I can tell you from personal experience that keeping track of your hours can be a bit of a pain. But you'll find that you do get in the habit of always checking the time before and after you work on a client file and making a note of it. That's why I like to switch my bookkeeping clients over to flat bookkeeping rates after I've done their books for a few months. This means after about three months of doing regular work for them, I'll come up with a flat rate and charge them that.

Usually by the third month of doing a client's books, I'll have a feel for how long it takes from start to finish. Each set of books has its own "personality" and it takes a while to become familiar with each one. Also, by then I'll have systems and "recurring entries" set up to make the job go more smoothly.

So to come up with this flat rate, just take an average of how long it takes you each month to do all the work required for each client; then add a little more as a buffer for year-end procedures and multiply by your hourly rate.

You can always adjust your flat rate up or down as needed at a later date.

Offering flat bookkeeping rates really is the best way to go when running your bookkeeping business because you don't have to keep track of your hours and you get paid the same amount each and every month.

Bookkeeping Services to Offer

Your next decision will be to decide on the services you will offer to your clients. Not all bookkeepers offer the same services. Here is a list of the basic services that most bookkeepers provide:

Accounts Payable
Post supplier invoices or checks (most clients write their own supplier checks and have you post them.)

Accounts Receivable
Posting of written invoices or daily sales totals to track revenue (spreadsheets are ideal for retail client daily sales transactions.)

Month End Transactions
Reconcile bank statement and post all monthly journal entries.

Financial Statements
Provide monthly Income Statement and Balance Sheet for client.

General Bookkeeping
- Posting all miscellaneous transactions.
- Accounting for all capital purchases.
- Preparing books for accountant at year-end.

Government Remittances
Ensure all government remittances are paid on time (some bookkeepers pay these at the bank for their clients.) Many bookkeepers offer a guarantee that remittances are paid on time or they pay the late charges.

Optional Services:

Payroll
- Not all bookkeepers offer this service as it requires considerable knowledge of employee and labor laws.
- Employees' paychecks are calculated with applicable deductions.
- Year-end tax forms are prepared (i.e. W-2's in the U.S., T4's in Canada.)

TIP: Some freelance bookkeepers prefer to use a payroll provider (such as ADP) rather than doing the payroll themselves. That way they simply have to input the hours and submit them to the payroll provider.

You'll find that doing bookkeeping for small clients will be very different from the bookkeeping you've probably done while working for an employer. Most companies you'll have worked for operate on a much larger scale. You'll learn more about how to do a small set of books in the "Monthly Bookkeeping" section on page 111.

Other Services to Offer

While you're planning your bookkeeping business, you should consider what other sources of revenue you could incorporate into your business to make it even more profitable.

Some people want to offer a full service administrative business while others would prefer to specialize in bookkeeping only. This decision will be based upon on your current skill level and the vision you have for your business.

Other services to consider including in your bookkeeping business are:

Word Processing/Secretarial Services

- Letters
- Forms
- Manuscripts
- Résumés
- Transcription

Data Entry

- Mailing Lists
- Databases

Desktop Publishing

- Brochures
- Fliers
- Newsletters

Virtual Assistant Services

- Everything listed above plus:
  o Article writing
  o Website design
  o Answering emails

Collections

- Collection reminder letters
- Collection phone calls

Tax Returns

- Personal income tax returns
- Business income tax returns

> **TIP:** If you plan to offer tax return services, make sure that you are up to date on the latest tax laws and have taken the required training for your local province or state.

Business Plan

All businesses need a business plan in order to succeed and a bookkeeping business is no different. A business plan is simply a road map of where you want your business to go.

Your business plan forces you to sit down and create the goals and vision of how you see your business growing over the next few years.

To most people, writing a business plan is the most stressful part about starting a business. Having to actually sit down and put all your ideas into printed form can be an intimidating task.

It doesn't have to be though. Once you have all the details down on paper that have been running around your head, you can finally relax and concentrate on the business itself. This is because you've now established the road map of where you want your business to go.

How to Write Your Business Plan

Work through your business plan slowly, one section at a time. Think about each bit of information and how you would like to apply it to your business. If there are sections that you're not ready to deal with at that particular time, just move onto the next one and come back to it later.

Don't attempt to write your entire plan in one sitting as this can be too overwhelming for many people. Just take each section one at a time, in small, manageable portions. Sit down for about an hour a night for several nights.

When you're finished, print out the whole plan and proofread it. You will probably find sections in your plan that you'll want to go back and edit.

Once you have your plan finished keep it handy and refer to it often. You can always go back to update your business plan later.

What Your Business Plan Should Include

Your business plan should include the following sections:

- Executive summary
- Confidentiality and recognition of risks
- Business overview
- Products and services
- Marketing strategy
- Management and staffing
- Regulatory issues
- Risks
- Implementation plan
- Financial plan

For an example of a completed bookkeeping business plan that you can use to help you create your own, go to:
www.startbookkeepingbusiness.net/book-resources/

When to Quit Your Day Job

At this point you're probably wondering how you can transition from your full-time job to running your own bookkeeping business. At what point should you quit your job?

Here's what I did personally to go from being employed to self-employed in less than twelve months.

First, I found a couple of clients and took care of their bookkeeping during my evenings and weekends. I found them just by talking to everyone I came in contact with, from casual acquaintances to accountants I met on the job.

Then, I cut back my full-time bookkeeping job to four days a week. It was a little scary, but with the extra money I was making on the side I was able to afford it.

I now had time to find and service more bookkeeping clients, so I actively searched for more clients during my "day off" when I wasn't working on client paperwork.

Before long, I had more bookkeeping clients than I had time, so I took another day off from my job. Now, I was fortunate in this regard. I realize that not everybody can do this. I had to convince my boss that I could still get the work done by working harder and more efficiently during the remaining three days a week I had at my job.

So how could this work in your situation? You might have to convince your boss to hire another bookkeeper part-time and job share with that person. This would actually make it easier for you to transition out of your job as your co-worker would be fully trained by the time you leave.

You'll have to be prepared to work evenings and weekends in order to get your freelance bookkeeping work done. So for the first year of this transition period, be prepared to work harder than you ever have before.

Then, once you have enough clients to substitute your income from your job, quit your job and run your bookkeeping business from home full-time.

Exit Strategy

Even though it seems a little strange to be planning an end to your bookkeeping business before it even begins, this is something you should be thinking about. Eventually, you'll want to retire or perhaps go into another field entirely.

So make sure you plan what will happen with your business if you decide to leave it. Will you refer your clients to another bookkeeper? Will you try to sell your business?

You also need to make sure that you have systems in place so that your clients are taken care of if something should happen to you. Consider putting together an "Instruction Manual" that contains critical information on the running of your business. That way whoever ends up stepping in can easily locate this information. You could include:

- Where client files are located (on your computer and throughout your office)
- Passwords
- Banking information
- Website login information
- Email login information
- Where your company financial information is located
- Contact information for your lawyer, accountant, etc.

- Information on outstanding debts (loans, lines of credit, etc.)

Make sure you include everything you can think of to help the person (i.e. typically your significant other) who may end up handling your business affairs. Take time now to consider this, as it could affect your family down the road.

Chapter 3: Implementing Systems

Plans are only good intentions
unless they immediately degenerate
into hard work.
Peter Drucker (1909 - 2005)

Implementing Systems

One of the first things you'll need to do when you're setting up your bookkeeping business is to plan how you intend to organize your clients' financial information.

You must have a system in place that will allow you to easily bounce between each client's set of books so you know instantly where you left off and what needs to be done.

This is essential because frequently you'll need clarification from your client about bookkeeping transactions that took place. When you call them, sometimes it can take a while for them to get back to you. By the time you finally get the information you requested, you have to be able to pick up where you left off, without having to spend a lot of time analyzing the transaction in question.

There will be times that you have a client calling you looking for specific information that you have to be able to put your fingers on at a moment's notice. Clients can be fickle; if they have to wait too long for information or suspect that you're in any way disorganized, they will quickly lose faith in you and potentially take their business elsewhere.

So how do you set up an organized freelance bookkeeping office? Keep reading below for the tried and true methods that have worked for me.

First of all, I set up each client with a binder. At the front of each binder are Client Binder Sheets (see the examples on the following four pages.)

Company Name: [   ]

Year End Date: _____

Linked Accounts: ☐ Vendor & Purchases (A/P – Accounts Payable)
 ☐ Customer & Sales (A/R – Accounts Receivable)
 ☐ Payroll
 ☐ Inventory Items

Receiver General Payroll Remittances ☐ No ☐ Yes, if yes,
 ☐ Monthly 15th

 ☐ Quarterly _____
 (Months Ending)
 ☐ Annually _____

GST Remittances ☐ No ☐ Yes, if yes,
 ☐ Monthly
 _____
 (Date)
 ☐ Quarterly _____
 (Months Ending)
 ☐ Annually _____

WCB Remittance ☐ No ☐ Yes, if yes,
 ☐ Monthly
 _____
 (Date)
 ☐ Quarterly _____
 (Months Ending)
 ☐ Annually _____

PST Remittance ☐ No ☐ Yes, if yes,
 ☐ Monthly
 _____
 (Date)
 ☐ Annually _____

Corporate Tax ☐ No ☐ Yes, if yes,
 ☐ Monthly
 _____
 (Date)
 ☐ Annually _____

Company Name: [   ]

CLIENT BINDER

At the front of each binder, include:
- These information sheets
- Chart of Accounts (to be reprinted as accounts are added)
- Current backup disk
- Special instructions regarding the client's account, i.e.
    - Prepaids to be expensed each month
    - Payroll dates and delivery requirements
    - Payroll accruals and reversals each month
    - Any other special instructions regarding the account

Every month print and include in binder when applicable:

Balance Sheet	To end of current period
Income Statement / Profit & Loss Statement	Year to Date and Current Month
Bank Reconciliation	One section for each bank account
General Ledger	For all accounts
General Journal	Request by Journal number (1st will be the next one after last month's report. Last will be last one in system.)
Accounts Payable Aged Summary	For Current Month
Accounts Receivable Details	For Current Month
Payroll	Copies of paychecks, Government remittances and reports.

Company Name: [   ]

⊞ CHECKLIST FOR CLIENT'S YEAR END:

ITEM	DESCRIPTION	YES	NO	COMMENTS
REPORTS	Trial Balance			
	Balance Sheet (to Y/E)			
	Income Statement (YTD)			
	Bank Reconciliation			
	General Journals			
	General Ledger			
	Accounts Payable Detail			
	Accounts Receivable Detail			
BANK	Statements for complete year			
	Check stubs for complete year			
	Next month statements and stubs			
TAXES	Copies of reports for complete year			
	Reconciliation form			
PAYROLL REMITTANCES	Last Month Report			
WCB	Last Month Report			
PURCHASES	Invoices for all Capital Purchases			
INSURANCE	Prepaids			
BACKUP DISK	2 sets of backup disks			
NEXT YEAR BINDER	Copy of year end bank recs for next month			
	These note pages transferred to the new year's binder			

Company Name: _____

SPECIAL INSTRUCTIONS REGARDING THIS ACCOUNT:

(blank lined form)

They're a little difficult to read here, but hopefully you can see that these Client Binder Sheets contain a great deal of information about each client.

They are a critical part of a good client organization system. You can tell at a glance when remittances are due, if there are any special notes, what typical procedures are done as well as have a year-end checklist for each client.

> **TIP:** For a copy of these forms that you can edit and use (in Word format), just go to: **www.startbookkeepingbusiness.net/book-resources/**

The rest of the binder has tabbed dividers to store the following:

- Bank reconciliation
- Balance sheet
- Income/Profit & loss statement
- General journal
- Accounts payable
- Accounts receivable
- General ledger (usually printed at year-end)

So each time a client's bookkeeping is complete for the month, the printouts are stored in each section of their individual binder.

This is handy to refer to so you can tell at a glance which month you've completed up to for each client (for various reasons, some clients tend to be further behind in their paperwork than others).

At year-end, just remove the Client Binder Sheets from the front of the binder and give the rest of the binder to the client along with bank statements and the accounting data CD.

File Systems

An organized filing system is critical for storing client paperwork in your office. You need a system that allows for easy retrieval.

The filing system I use is organized by "client name" so all client files are kept together in one drawer. That way you can have more than one client file per drawer, which saves on space. Simply mark each client section by placing the client name on a tab that sits on the hanging file folder.

Within the client's "section" each file folder is color-coded. That way when you're looking for information, you can easily find it.

The files in this system are color coded and labeled as follows:

- <u>Current</u> – A yellow-colored file containing all new invoices, bank statements, etc. that the client has just brought in. By keeping all new information here for each client until you're ready to work on it, you help keep your desk and office uncluttered. You just need to pull out the "Current" file to see what work needs to done for the client.

- <u>Capital Purchases</u> – Another yellow file where all capital purchase invoices are placed so that they can be easily accessed at year-end.

- <u>Government</u> – Red file(s) containing all government remittance forms. This includes taxes, Worker's Compensation, and payroll remittances. Label a separate red file for each government remittance.

- <u>Bank Statement</u> – Blue file(s) containing all bank statements and canceled checks. You need one blue file for each bank account and for merchant credit card statements.

- <u>Sales/Revenue</u> – Green file(s) containing all sales invoices and sales summary sheets. You may want to have a separate green file for each customer the client has.

- <u>Accounts Payable</u> – Manila folders that are organized in an A to Z file system for the client's vendors. For smaller businesses this can be grouped together as A to M and N to Z, depending upon the number of venders the client deals with. For really small clients, simply put all invoices together in one Accounts Payable file.

Computer File Systems

Your computer accounting data for each client must be organized in a system that makes it simple to use. You don't want to waste the client's valuable time when you're billing them at $25 to $75 per hour.

You may have more than one year's data for each client on your computer system so you should have a good system in place to avoid confusion. You don't want to accidentally post into previous years' data (or into another client's data files!)

Here's an easy way to do this:

1. In your computer data directory, set up one data file for all company bookkeeping files. For example, you could name it: "Bookkeeping Data." Then subdivide this file into the following subfolders:

Eg.

- A to C
- D to F
- G to I

- J to L
- M to O
- P to R
- S to U
- W to Z

2. Then under the correct letter series, set up a company file for each client:

Eg.

- A to C
  - AAA Heating
  - B & C Janitorial
  - Central Plumbing

3. Then under each company file, set up subfolders for the "Year" file for all accounting data and an "Admin" file for all letters, spreadsheets, etc.

Eg.

- A to C
  - AAA Heating
    - 2008
    - 2009
    - 2010
    - Admin

4. Under each "Year," set up the client's current accounting data for that year:

Eg.

- A to C
  - AAA Heating
    - 2008

- AAA Heating 2008
  - 2009
    - AAA Heating 2009
  - 2010
    - AAA Heating 2010
  - Admin
    - Cash Expenses
    - Revenue Summary

You will be adding to this folder at the end of each year-end and setting up a new year to keep that company's accounting data.

It's important to keep each accounting year separate rather than continuing to use the same accounting file. Most accounting systems will only allow you to search the previous two year's data and you may need to search further back at some point in the future.

You will probably only want to keep four to five years data on your computer system depending upon your available data space. Anything beyond that, clients will have on their CD disks of data attached to their binders for the year in question.

Backup Systems

In order to protect your clients' data (and your own professional credibility) you need to have a couple of data backup systems in place in case of a computer system crash or disaster (fire, theft, flood, computer viruses, etc.)

You *must* have a plan in place as ALL computers will fail at some time or another. You risk losing your business if you don't have all your computer files backed up.

As mentioned earlier, you should have a current backup CD for each client at the front of their binder. After you complete your month end transactions for your client, pop in this disk and do a backup. It only takes a couple of minutes and could save you a nightmare of recreating data from source documents if you're ever faced with this.

However, you should have another backup system in place as CDs can frequently fail and should not be used as your sole backup source.

You should have your entire computer data stored off-site as well. One convenient way to do this is to use an online data backup system.

Over the last few years online backup systems have become a reliable and inexpensive way to protect your data. With faster Internet connections, backing up over the Internet can now be done safely and effectively.

I personally use Carbonite, which is an online backup system. In fact, only a few months after I installed the program, it saved me when my computer crashed and could not be restored.

Carbonite encrypts all backup data, so it's completely secure. It's inexpensive to use and easy to set up. The program backs up your data automatically, so you don't even have to think about it.

The first backup can take the longest as you have to go through your system and manually select the files you want to backup (although they may have automated this process now). It can take a couple of days to complete the backup depending on how much data you're backing up.

> **TIP:** To back up your bookkeeping files, simply right-click on your "Bookkeeping Data" folder where all your client sub-folders are kept, then select "Carbonite – Backup".

You also need to always have the most current virus and spyware software installed on your computer to protect your data. Make sure you set this up so it runs *daily*.

It's just too easy to pick up viruses these days so you must make sure that you take steps to combat this threat to your computer's data.

Typical Bookkeeping Routine

It's difficult to give you a detailed description of what each day will be like because when you have dozens of clients on the go, you will be jumping from client to client a great deal throughout the day.

Some days you may be working on one client's books all day while another day you may be completing transactions for several different clients throughout the day. Being able to confidently bounce from client-to-client in an organized fashion will save you from unnecessary stress in your workday.

Nevertheless, here's a brief rundown of the steps you might take when doing month-end transactions for a client using the systems outlined in this book:

1. Pull out the client's information (bank statements, invoices, receipts, etc.) from their yellow "Current" file folder.

2. Take out the client's binder.

3. Review notes on starter pages as a reminder of any necessary information for that client.

4. Open your accounting program data file on your computer for the current year for that client by going to your "Bookkeeping Data" file.

5. Do all your bookkeeping transactions for the month for the client (bank reconciliation, post sales, post cash-paid receipts, post invoices, etc.)

6. When everything balances, print off your Balance Sheet, Income Statement, Bank Reconciliation, Journal Entries, Accounts Payable Summary, and Account Receivable Summary for the month. Hole-punch and place in the client binder in each tabbed section.

7. Do a backup onto your client's CD, which should be located at the front of the binder.

8. File away all bank statements, receipts, invoices, etc. into the applicable colored file folders.

9. Update your "Client Working List" (see page 103.)

Setting Boundaries and Office Hours

If you're not setting boundaries in your bookkeeping business, you will find yourself getting burned out rather quickly.

You'll find that some bookkeeping clients automatically assume that because you're working at home they can call you whenever they want...evenings, weekends, or late at night.

They'll call with a "Sorry to bother you but I have a quick question" or "Can you look this up for me?" Before you know it, you're working during your time off.

This can get very irritating because you still have your own personal life and your family's needs to attend to. You work hard and deserve a break from your business during your off hours. It's very easy to fall into this trap when you're self-employed.

If you don't train your clients to call you only during your office hours, they *will* call you all the time, guaranteed. So your first step is to inform your clients of when you'll be in the office to take calls.

> **TIP:** This is a double-edged sword though, because sometimes when you're working in the office, you don't want to be disturbed if you're in the middle of doing some intense number crunching. That's when voicemail is such a blessing. Make sure you call your client back as soon as you're able to take a break from your task.

The next step in training your clients is to absolutely not answer your phone during non-business hours unless it's an emergency (and it never is). If you start answering your clients' phone calls during your non-working hours even once, you open the door for them to do it again. Don't risk it. Let them leave a message and call them back during your office hours.

This goes for answering emails and faxes from clients during your non-business hours as well. If they're sending you work (such as payroll) and they get it to you after office hours, you'll have to make a tough call on whether you'll put it off until your next work day or not.

I've personally made sure all my clients know that I absolutely don't work weekends. So if they don't get me their payroll on time, it has to wait until Monday. They are all very understanding about my policy, and this has eliminated much of the problem.

If you don't train your clients, they will train you... to be at their beck and call. So set your boundaries in your bookkeeping business from the start.

Confidentiality

As a freelance bookkeeper who is entrusted with sensitive financial information about your clients, it's extremely important that you treat all client information as strictly confidential. This means not discussing any aspects of the identity of your other clients or their financial situations with anybody.

Even an offhand remark about another client can come back to haunt you. Clients will wonder if you are telling other people about their private information.

If you have clients visiting your office, make sure there are no other client files open or lying around where they can be read by others. For this reason, it may make more sense to meet with clients at your kitchen table or in your living room.

Your business reputation is at stake, so make sure you guard all of your clients' information at all times.

Finding Balance Working at Home

Another problem that is common to freelance bookkeepers is how easy it is to become a workaholic. This is a problem that I still struggle with, and there are no easy solutions.

It's important to stick to your office hours and force yourself to close your office door at the end of your day. You don't want to neglect your family and other personal obligations just because you are building your business.

It is very difficult to find a good balance between work and home life. Since you're working in the same place where you play with the kids, cook dinner, and do your housework, it's hard to separate the two. That's when you wind up doing laundry when you should be finishing a client's books, or spending your evening working because you decided to check your email.

Once you have a schedule in place, do your best to stick to it. Set some rules for the rest of the family. Make sure they know that you expect their support. Conversely, have them hold you accountable if you are working too much so that you don't end up burning out or becoming a workaholic.

Finding Your Motivation

Motivating yourself to excel in your bookkeeping business should not be something you do only when the spirit moves you. It's an ongoing process that should include every facet of your business life—your mental attitude, physical well-being and appearance, work atmosphere, interaction with clients, and off-the-job environment.

So how can you stay motivated? Here are some tips:

Maintain a Positive Attitude

We are all responsible for our own actions and attitudes, and changing them when appropriate. When you're around people or things that are uplifting and positive, you feel that way. You have more confidence in yourself and know that you can change whatever needs changing. If you can make your workplace such a place you'll find you feel happier and more productive.

Create Positive Affirmations

The reason for writing goals for your bookkeeping business is the same as creating positive affirmations on paper. What your eyes see and ears hear, your mind will believe.

After you've written them down, read them aloud to yourself – and do it every morning when you get into your office. You'll be amazed at what happens. Come up with a set of new ones every month. Statements such as, "I'm an important and valuable person," or "I know I'll make good use of my time today." Repeating them out loud everyday at a set time will help reinforce positive actions.

Get Some Exercise Every Day

Make sure you get up and walk around your desk or office throughout the day. Maybe you can go outside to get the mail and enjoy the sunlight, or just get up and do a few stretches.

Concentrated, tense thinking makes all your muscles tighten up. So periodic stretching, even at your desk, or just getting up and walking over to the window and getting a different view can help.

It only takes a little concentrated effort on your part to keep motivated and productive, which will lead to success in your bookkeeping business.

Chapter 4: Marketing Your Business

"It seems to me that people have vast potential. Most people can do extraordinary things if they have the confidence or take the risks. Yet most people don't. They sit in front of the telly and treat life as if it goes on forever."

Philip Adams

Advertising

Promoting your bookkeeping business is one of the most important tasks that you must do. After all, without clients, you don't have a business.

There are many methods of advertising. Some will work better than others. So make sure you mix and match and try out some of these methods.

Plan your advertising budget and break it down choosing a variety of advertising media. Do not skimp on your advertising budget.

Branding

Branding your business is more than just creating a logo. Your brand represents the impression that potential clients get when they think of your business. To create your brand you must understand your clients' needs and values. This is the professional image that you envisioned while writing your business plan.

Creating a brand for your business is not just for large corporations. Small home-based businesses need brand recognition as much as, if not more so, than big companies.

You don't need to spend thousands of dollars to create your brand, you simply need to be consistent and use it throughout your marketing materials. Branding is a combination of everything your bookkeeping business uses to present itself.

Here are a few important elements to branding your business:

1. Your logo, stationery, website and advertising should all look professionally designed and be easy to understand.

2. Create a tagline that is used consistently throughout your advertising.

3. Customer service is critical so make sure all your communications with clients reinforces your professional image.

4. Make sure you let potential clients know what differentiates you from your competitors.

Take a good look at your bookkeeping business strengths and benefits. Then make sure your branding strategy (marketing materials, advertising, sales, customer service, logo, etc.) reinforces this.

Sales Letters

Writing a sales letter to potential clients is an extremely effective way to immediately let them discover your services. This should be your first advertising medium of choice with all other advertising media (display ads, postcards, newsletters, etc.) being follow-ups.

This advertising medium gives you the opportunity to let your potential clients find out who you are, what you can do, and most importantly, how it will benefit them.

Using a word processing program such as Microsoft Word, you can quickly do a mail merge to send out personalized letters to hundreds of businesses at a time.

This is a great way to introduce your business; however, don't expect a *huge* response from just using this method alone. The average success rate for using direct mailing alone is 1 percent. By following up each letter with a phone call, this percentage can rise to about 5 percent.

If you don't like "cold calling" (and who does?) your other choice is to follow up your sales letter with these advertising methods:

- Display ad
- Classified ad
- Newsletter
- Postcard

To help get you started, on the following page is a sales letter that I used that received a 3 percent response rate. Use it as a starting point to create your own letter.

Date

AAA Heating
123 Main Street
Anytown

Dear Sir / Madam:

You may have discovered while you've been operating AAA Heating that you are in need of a bookkeeper. I would like to offer my assistance. With over 12 years of experience, "ABC Bookkeeping Services" provides excellent bookkeeping support.

You can have access to bookkeeping services such as:

- Your vendor checks professionally printed out and mailed
- Payroll for your employees
- Your government remittances paid on time
- Posting and printing your invoices
- Your monthly financial statements to show how AAA Heating is doing
- Collection letters for your slow paying clients

I have been instrumental in helping other businesses in this area reach maximum success.   I look forward to the opportunity of working with you and bringing about AAA's Heating's financial future.

Please call 555-123-4567 or email abcbookkeeping@email.com to receive our free information package.

Sincerely,

Your name

Mailing Lists

In order to do your mailing campaigns, you'll need to put together a mailing list to send out your sales letters, newsletters, and postcards. This can be done a couple of different ways: by renting a list from a list broker or by creating one yourself.

Renting a mailing list of business owners can cost anywhere from $100 and up. Look in your local Yellow Pages under "Advertising – Direct Mail." You can also do an online search for list brokers.

Alternatively, you can develop a list for free by spending some time researching potential businesses in your local area. If you're starting out on a tight budget, I recommend taking this approach because the only thing it will cost you is your time.

You can put together this list using:

- Your local telephone book
- Chamber of Commerce member list
- City Hall business license directory

You may need to use a combination of all three to get all the information you require. You will need the following for your mailing list:

- Contact name
- Business name
- Address
- Zip/postal code

- Telephone number (if you plan to follow up with a phone call)

Logo

In order to create your brand for your business, you should develop a logo.

If you're creative, this can be done quite simply using a program such as Microsoft Publisher. If you're not very creative, you may need to find a graphic designer who can produce one for you.

Alternatively, if you have a college or university nearby, you could hire a student to create a logo at a much cheaper rate than the cost of hiring a professional graphic designer.

Your logo represents the company image that you're trying to portray. To develop yours, start by writing out some words that best represent what you want clients to visualize when they see your logo. These will probably be similar words that you came up with when you named your business.

Here are some ideas to get you started:

- Honesty
- Ethical
- Accuracy
- Reliable

After you've done this, try to come up with some images that represent these words. It may take some time but give this exercise a try.

For instance, if you wanted to convey the word "wisdom," you might want to use the image of an owl.

It's essential that you establish your image, or "brand." Your brand should be repeated throughout all of your advertising. You want people to know immediately when they see your logo exactly who you are, what you do and what you stand for.

Yellow Pages

You will most likely get a lot of your business from a Yellow Pages ad as most people turn to this resource first when seeking a bookkeeper. However, you must have a business telephone line to be listed in the Yellow Pages, and this can be very expensive when you're first starting out.

You also can only place your ad once a year, so you may have to wait a considerable amount of time before you're able to get into the next printing.

On the following pages are some great advertising methods to use in conjunction to, or while you're waiting for, your Yellow Pages ad to come out.

Display Ads

Display ads can be an effective way to get your bookkeeping business noticed if done in conjunction with sales letters.

One drawback to display ads, however, is that they can be expensive. Daily newspapers are obviously more costly than weekly papers. Call around to get a rate quote from your local newspapers.

Negotiate a volume discount with the advertising rep from the newspaper. Inquire what their rates would be if you were to run an ad consistently over a period of time, for example, three days in a row or three weekends in a row.

If you manage to get a decent advertising rate, develop a small display ad and run it repeatedly.

Make sure that you always request a final proof of the ad before it runs. Check it over carefully for errors and then give your final approval to the newspaper. This way if there are any errors you can have the newspaper rerun the ad at no extra charge to you.

To make your display ad more interesting you may want to consider creating a "Question and Answer" type display ad using a different question each time you run it. People will be more likely to read this type of ad out of curiosity, especially if you answer bookkeeping questions potential clients may have.

On the following page is an example of some "Question and Answer" display ads that I ran that did quite well.

Come up with a variety of questions and you could easily run these ads weekly.

TIP: You'll find a Microsoft Publisher version of these ads by going to:
  www.startbookkeepingbusiness.net/book-resources/

Ask the Bookkeeping Pro

ABC Bookkeeping Services

Tel: 555-123-4567
Email: abcbookkeeping@email.com

Q. How can I keep track of all the money coming in and out of my business bank account?

A. A Cashflow sheet is the easiest way to keep track of your inflows and outflows of cash. A good Cashflow sheet will give you an instant snapshot of your money situation. A Cashflow sheet is set up on a spreadsheet such as Excel and can be tracked on a weekly or monthly basis. Ask your bookkeeper for a sample of a Cashflow sheet or have them set one up for you.

Our Services:

- **Payroll**
- **Accounts Payable & Receivable**
- **General Bookkeeping**
- **Small Business & Tax Returns**
- **Government Remittances**

Ask the Bookkeeping Pro

ABC Bookkeeping Services

Tel: 555-123-4567
Email: abcbookkeeping@email.com

Q. Do I still need a bookkeeper if I know how to use an accounting program?

A. There is more to bookkeeping than just inputting your data. You must know how to post items correctly . For example, some items can be classified as assets and depreciated and some should be posted as an expense against income.   These are situations that a trained bookkeeper will know and can actually save you money. Correcting numerous posting errors at year end will mean paying a higher accountant's bill than necessary.

Our Services:

- **Payroll**
- **Accounts Payable & Receivable**
- **General Bookkeeping**
- **Small Business & Tax Returns**
- **Government Remittances**

Classified Ads

People love to read the classified ad section of the newspaper. By listing your classified ad under "Services for Hire" or some other such heading, potential clients will easily find your ad.

The trick, however, is to write a catchy headline that will make people stop to read your ad. You also need to get your point across in as few words as possible because you're being charged by the word.

Experiment with this and try out several different ads. Also, look at ads other people are running to see how they're worded. If you see the same ad being run consistently week after week, you can bet that the person running it is seeing results from that ad. Use this ad as a springboard to develop your own winning ad.

If your first classified ad doesn't pull any responses, you can usually change the wording before the next newspaper issue.

Remember that you are trying to increase the number of times that people see your ad in combination with your other advertising methods, so don't be too disappointed if you don't get too many phone calls from your first classified ad.

Here's a very simple classified ad:

Bookkeeping Service

Government Remittances, Payroll, General Bookkeeping

Reliable, 10 years experience. Call 555-1122

Craigslist

Many freelance bookkeepers are turning to Craigslist.org to advertise their business. And why not? Craigslist is free to use (in most areas) and many people actively visit this online resource daily.

Craigslist is an online community where users can exchange information, buy or sell items, seek jobs, or even find friends or romantic partners.

Simply go to the "Services – Financial" section on the city of your choice and place your ad. There is no need to worry about word limits, as it's free. However, make sure your ad is clear and easy to understand.

Referrals from Accountants

The most effective (and cheapest) way to get business is from referrals. By developing a relationship with the accountants in your area you will rapidly be the first person the accountant calls when their clients need help with their day-to-day bookkeeping.

Accountants are <u>always</u> looking for good bookkeepers to refer their clients to. It makes the accountant look good and saves them from an accounting nightmare at year-end.

Contact your local accounting firms to find out which accountant handles subcontracting and referrals for bookkeeping services.

Start by writing each accountant an individual letter introducing yourself and your company. Make sure you follow up with a phone call to arrange to meet with them. Some firms may request a copy of your résumé detailing your work experience, so make sure you have yours updated and ready to send to them.

Make sure you follow up with each individual accountant on a regular basis, either by phoning them or by writing follow up letters to setup a meeting.

> **TIP:** You may even want to invite them out for lunch so they can get to know you better.

Joining Business Groups

Consider joining your local Chamber of Commerce, Rotary Club, or other business networking group. These groups usually have regular networking meetings or events so people in business can make contact with one another. Make sure you attend as many business functions as you can.

Networking can be difficult if you tend to be shy but do make an effort to meet as many people as possible. Try to relax and just have fun with it.

Challenge yourself to hand out a certain number of business cards every time you go. Even if you meet people who clearly are not in the market for a bookkeeper, don't prejudge or dismiss them. Just because a person is not looking for a bookkeeper right at the moment doesn't mean that they won't keep your business card and refer you to someone they know down the road.

Have an "elevator speech" ready for when you meet a prospective client. An elevator speech is your "30 second sound bite" introducing who you are and what you do.

For example:

> "My name is Susan Jones. I'm a freelance bookkeeper who assists small businesses by handling their finances so they can relax and take care of their business."

The idea of your elevator speech is to list a benefit your client enjoys by doing business with you. In the example above, the benefit would be "so they can relax and take care of their business." Consider the benefit you want your clients to have and incorporate this into your elevator speech.

Make sure you have your elevator speech memorized so that it flows easily.

Newsletters

A newsletter is an effective way to quietly remind customers about your bookkeeping services after you have sent your initial sales letter. They are generally a welcome piece of mail and not as likely to be immediately tossed away.

Newsletters contain information relevant to potential clients' businesses and, as such, are more likely to be read and kept longer than other forms of advertising.

By using a desktop publishing program (such as Publisher) it's now easier than ever to create a professional looking newsletter. By using the templates in Publisher, all you have to do is fill in a few text boxes and voilà, you're done.

If you have a talent for writing and coming up with topics for newsletter articles, you should have no trouble filling up a small two page newsletter.

If you're looking for topic ideas, a great way to discover what information people are looking for is to check out the various business newsgroups on the Internet. You can also take topics from articles that have already been written and put your own spin on these ideas.

If, however, you find yourself short of articles (and time) for your newsletter, there is an easier way to fill up your newsletter. Copyright free articles are available online at such sites as:

- http://www.EzineArticles.com
- http://www.GoArticles.com

These articles can be freely used as long as the writer's name and contact information are included at the bottom of the article. Some writers also request that you send a sample copy of your newsletter to them.

By cutting and pasting these articles into your newsletter, you can easily create a full newsletter in hours, not days.

Make sure that your newsletter has an ad or article promoting your own business as well. But don't place your information directly on the front page as your readers may decide that your newsletter is simply a glorified ad and stop reading.

When you name the newsletter, use a name that relates to your business name. For example, if your business name is "ABC Bookkeeping Services," you could name your newsletter "ABC Ledger" or "ABC Journal Entry." This will help keep your business name (and brand) in front of your potential customers.

You will want to create a newsletter that is as interesting and informative to your reader as possible. You'll have about five seconds after they open it to catch your readers' attention with your newsletter. So make the first page really grab them by the lapels.

Consider what kinds of topics your potential client will be interested in learning more about.

Here are some ideas:

- Advertising/Marketing

- Insurance

- Customer relations

- Success strategies

- Simple bookkeeping tips

- Home business tips

Postcards

Postcards are an inexpensive and quick way to remind potential clients of your bookkeeping services. Due to their unusual shape and size, the recipient is more apt to read them as long as you make them eye-catching.

Use them only after you've established initial contact with your sales letter to remind your contacts who you are.

Using a desktop publishing program (such as Publisher) you can create four postcards on one cardstock sheet. By making one cut vertically and one horizontally, you now have four postcards. You can cut them yourself or have them done at your local print shop after they're photocopied.

You can use brightly colored cardstock to make your postcards really stand out.

The front of the postcard should have something catchy such as a humorous graphic design or the Question & Answer format (from the Display Ad section on page 82) to further tie your advertising message together.

On the back side, list your business name, logo, phone number, email address, and website along with a list of the services you provide.

TIP: Want to really make your postcards stand out and get attention? Take a digital picture of your potential client's business and use that as the front of your postcard!

Website

Having a website to showcase your bookkeeping business is important in several ways:

- It's extremely cheap advertising (you just pay monthly web hosting fees after you've purchased your domain name).

- You can post information on your services, rates, and other related bookkeeping information so that when potential customers call, most of their questions are already answered (i.e. they are already presold on your services.)

- Having your bookkeeping website listed and linked onto local business directories can usually be done for free.

Here are some examples of bookkeeping websites for you to check out for ideas. Notice how each site is set up and what type of information is provided.

http://www.NYCBookkeepers.com/

http://www.InTheBlackBooks.com/index.html

http://www.VirtualBookkeeping.ca/

If you want to look at local bookkeeping websites for ideas, go to http://www.Google.com and type in the keyword:

"*city* +bookkeeping"

Enter your own *city* and check out what your bookkeeping competitors are doing.

Options to Consider Adding to Your Website:

- An auto-responder to collect names and email addresses so you can send prospects updates, newsletters, and other related information. (I suggest **Aweber.com** for this.)

- Links to sites containing information business owners need such as government sites, tax information, etc.

- Testimonials, if you have them, from clients or former employers.

- Articles on topics that your potential clients would find useful.

Options to <u>Avoid</u> Adding To Your Website:

1) Background Music

Stay away from looping background music onto your site. It might sound pleasant to you at first, but if you run a website with several pages and every time a visitor browses to another page on your site, the background music starts playing again, you'll find most visitors will just leave your site.

2) Extra Large/Small Text Size

There is more to web design than purely graphics—user accessibility is one big part of it too! You should design the text on your site to be legible and reasonably sized to enable your visitors to read it without straining their eyes. No matter how good the content of your website or your sales copy is, if it's illegible people will be turned off.

3) Popup Windows

Popup windows are blatantly used to display advertisements. I close them automatically every time one manages to pass through my popup blocker. Imagine if you had a very important message to convey and you put it in a popup window that gets killed most of the time it appears on a visitor's screen. Your website loses its function immediately.

What Your Website Should Have

Your website does not have to be huge. Here are the pages that your website must have:

Home Page

- This is your welcome page that offers highlights of your business and what it can do for the client
- You can list your phone number or email address here if you like
- You can include a photo (headshot) of yourself here

Services Page

- This is where you get to show your stuff
- List all your services here

Rates Page

- Although this page is optional and some people prefer not to use it (I personally believe it deters tire-kickers and time-wasters)
- List your hourly rates and state if you offer flat rates

Testimonials Page

- This page is optional as well but will really help to pre-sell you using the benefits of "social proof"

- You can use testimonials from clients or letters from employers here

About Page

- This is where you state all your education, training, and experience

- You can provide some personal information but try to focus mainly on your business experience

- You should have a headshot of yourself here

TIP: An easy way to create your own website is to simply use WordPress and set it up on your own hosting account with a good domain name.

Marketing Kit

When clients respond to your advertising message, whether it's by phone or email, you need to be able to follow up with an informative marketing kit that includes complete details about your bookkeeping business. This kit contains the following information:

- Your biographical profile

- Your company description
- Vision statement (from your business plan)
- Mission statement (also from business plan)
- Fact sheet
- Your guarantee
- A headshot photo of yourself

Your business marketing kit reinforces your advertising message and gives the potential client further background information on your bookkeeping business.

Marketing kit sheets should be placed into a two-pocket portfolio folder along with your brochure and business card. A large label with your business name and logo on the front will also add a professional touch.

If you have a website in place, you can forego this marketing kit (which can be expensive to produce) and instead direct potential clients to your website.

TIP: For samples of this marketing kit, go to our website and download it here:
www.startbookkeepingbusiness.net/book-resources/

Chapter 5: Client Maintenance

Real integrity is doing the right thing, knowing that nobody's going to know whether you did it or not.

Oprah Winfrey, in Good Housekeeping

Invoicing Clients

You'll find the most exciting part of being a freelance bookkeeper is creating an invoice and then receiving a check for it. Even though typing up invoices can be a bit tedious (as it's part of the tasks that you may do for clients anyway), it's very rewarding when you receive payment.

You can do your client invoices monthly, bi-weekly, or for whatever period you prefer. Some bookkeepers invoice right away when a job is complete rather than waiting until the next invoice period. That way they can submit the invoice to the client at the same time they meet with them to discuss details and hand over paperwork.

If you have worked with a client for a while, you'll find that invoicing with a flat monthly rate (as discussed on page 42) will make it much simpler to create your invoices. You can even set up a recurring entry for this so it's essentially just a matter of printing the invoice.

Credit Policies

You will want to establish a credit policy to ensure that you receive prompt payment from clients. You can offer "30 days" on your invoices but as a small home business owner, you'll be better off if you state that your invoices are "Due Upon Receipt." Many small businesses require this, and there is no reason that you should have to wait thirty days or more to receive payment for your work.

However, make sure your credit policy is stated clearly on your invoice and in your contract with your clients so there's no misunderstanding as to when you expect to be paid.

Avoiding Late Payments

Once your credit policies are established, there are a couple of ways to prevent clients from paying your monthly invoices late.

First of all, if possible, give your invoice to your client in person at the same time you present them with their completed monthly paperwork. Place the invoice right on top of the paperwork so that your client can't miss it. Many times, they'll pay it immediately.

If you don't receive payment within the first week, give your client a phone call. Often you won't even have to mention the invoice; your client will bring it up and let you know when you can expect a check. If they don't mention it, however, politely ask when the check will be ready. You could even offer to pick it up.

Generally, if you train your clients from the start to expect you to follow up if they don't pay promptly, most will be sure to cut a check right away to avoid you calling them.

Forms of Payment

You'll find that if you have several ways of accepting payments from your clients, this will also increase your likelihood of getting paid faster.

I suggest that you use PayPal as a payment processor for an excellent alternative to cash or checks. With PayPal, clients can choose to pay with available cash or use their credit card. This makes it an easy way for you to accept credit cards without having the hassle of setting up an expensive merchant account.

There are some small fees for using PayPal, so make sure you take this into account. However, the convenience can't be beat.

Retainers

Before you begin work on any new set of books, you may want to consider requesting a retainer fee upfront from the client. This is to ensure that you get paid until you become familiar with the client's payment practices.

Getting a retainer can save you a great deal of time and money if, down the road, you discover that your client has a habit of not paying his or her creditors.

Asking for a retainer is common practice among bookkeepers, accountants, and lawyers so you don't need to feel self-conscious about requesting one. Simply state that you require a retainer before you can begin work on the client's books.

If you do have a client who has questionable bill paying practices, keep requesting a retainer as the work progresses. When one retainer has been used up, don't do any more work until your client submits a new one. Then you'll never find yourself having to "carry" any outstanding accounts receivables from your clients.

A retainer can be anywhere from $100 to $500 (or more) depending upon the size of the job. If you will be doing a great deal of bookkeeping (such as a year's worth of data) for a company, you may want to request a larger amount.

Raising Your Rates

You will want to re-evaluate your hourly rates each year to make sure that they are competitive and your profit margins are being met. This does not mean that you should automatically raise your rates every year, but you should keep an eye on them. It doesn't hurt to phone around again to other bookkeepers and verify hourly rates after an extended length of time has gone by.

Most clients will grumble when you raise your rates. However, if you only increase them by a few dollars per hour, many clients will be fine with that.

Your clients will appreciate either a short letter or a phone call if you do raise your rates. Don't just raise them by adjusting your invoices.

This is why is it so important to make sure that the rates you set when you start your business are reasonable. It's very hard to raise your rates in steep increments once your clients are used to paying a certain amount. You may lose some clients if you do a large increase in your hourly rates.

Tracking Billable Hours

Keeping track of your billable hours is critical for both you and your client. If you're not accurately doing this you could end up not getting paid for work that you've done.

Time tracking can be a short-term task that can be eliminated once a client has been established for a few months. If you're charging by the hour, you'll need an accurate record of the hours spent on each client's books.

There are many ways to keep track of your billable hours, but here are three of the most popular methods for bookkeeping businesses:

1.   Use Your Client's File

This is a simple way of tracking time by just taking note of all your start and finish times and recording them on a piece of paper taped to the inside of your client's "Current" file folder.

You can use a separate piece of paper for each month or just do a running balance and total it at the end of each month. Your hours will all be kept together in one place and you can show them to your client should the need ever arise.

2.   Use Your Accounting Program

Some accounting programs have a time tracking feature that allows you to record the stop and finish times for client work. This sounds good in theory but has some drawbacks.

First, you have to have your own bookkeeping business accounting books open at the same time you have your clients' books open.

Second, some accounting programs limit this feature to employee use only, which excludes you as a small business owner.

Finally, the finished invoices that are produced have a whole list of confusing start and finish times that will inevitably confuse your bookkeeping client and create possible problems.

3. Use a Day-Timer

This is my favorite method of tracking time for a bookkeeping business. You simply need a Day-Timer that has either one page per day or three days to a page. I've used both and they both work equally well; the amount of space just depends on how many clients you work on per day.

This method means you have all your hours recorded in a book that you can easily keep for as long as you want. So if there is ever a dispute over hours worked, you have a handy record that you can produce.

Enter your start and finish times as you work on each client's books. Also, make a brief note of what you did during that session.

This may seem cumbersome at first but after a few days of doing this, it becomes a habit.

For example, your daily diary could look something like this:

July 12
9 to 10:15 - B & C Janitorial – payroll - 1.25
10:15 to 12:00 - Central Plumbing – June month end - 1.75
12:30 to 3:00 - AAA Heating – accounts payable - 2.5
3:00 to 4:30 - XYZ Trading – meeting with new client - 1.5

Not only does this give you a daily diary of the hours you've put into each client's books, but it also gives you a brief summary of what you did for the client if they should ever question their invoice from you.

You'll find your own style and abbreviations that work for you. Make sure you also record your non-billable hours that you spend on your own business transactions (such as your advertising, bookkeeping, etc.) for each day as well. That way you can track where all your time is going.

At the end of every day, your billable hours should be transferred from your daily diary to a "Client Billing Form" spreadsheet. This spreadsheet will contain the hours worked for each client which is then totaled at month end.

Then when you do your month-end client billing, all you have to do is take the total hours from the "Client Billing Form" and enter them into your accounting invoice for that client. It's as simple as that.

Keeping track of your hours daily may seem time-consuming at first, but it actually only takes a few minutes and is a pleasant way to finish off your day. It's important to keep on top of this each day, while the information is still fresh in your mind.

This spreadsheet is set up so it adds up total hours worked and allows you to bill your client at the end of each month. See the example below:

Jan-10	1	2	3	4	5	6	7	8	9	10	to month end Total
AAA Heating	0.25				1				1		2.25
B & C Janitorial		0.25		1.25			0.25	2		1.5	5.25
Central Plumbing				1.75		2				0.75	4.5
D & L Motors	3	2		0.25	1				2		8.25

Tracking Client Progress

You will need to develop a system to keep track of the bookkeeping work that's been completed for each client on an ongoing basis.

One way to do this is to set up a "Client Working List" spreadsheet detailing the services provided to each client. Make sure you keep this spreadsheet up to date after you complete each task.

I find just by going through the "Client Working List" a couple of times a week that I know what has been completed and I can easily keep on top of my clients' deadlines.

By entering the date each transaction was completed you know instantly the status of each client. This information is invaluable when you have many clients and you need to keep track of critical time-sensitive deadlines for each client.

For example, after you finished the March Payroll Remittance for AAA Heating, you would enter the date you completed it, i.e. April 15.

See circled item in the "Client Working List" example below:

ABC Bookkeeping Services
Accounts
Monthly / Annual Report Checklist

AAA Heating	Comment	Date completed	Jan	Feb	Mar	Apr
Year End Dec. 31						
George Smith		Tax Remittance				
555-1234		Payroll Remittance		15-Feb	15-Mar	(15-Apr)
Accountant: Bob Jones		WCB	5-Jan			
		Bank Reconciliation		15-Feb	20-Mar	25-Apr
		Month End Reports Printed		15-Feb	20-Mar	25-Apr
		W-2's				
		Year End to Accountant				

> **TIP:** See the "Client Working List" spreadsheet located at
> **www.startbookkeepingbusiness.net/book-resources/**

Tracking Expenses

Keeping track of day to day expenses incurred for each client will help ensure that you are still making a profit in your bookkeeping business. These types of expenses include envelopes, stamps, binders, and photocopies.

You can either bill your clients separately for these items or work them into your hourly rate.

To track these items, set up a spreadsheet that is labeled with "Binder," "Stamps," "Envelopes," and "Photocopies" across the top and list clients' names down the side of the page.

Then, whenever you pull out a new binder, send a document, or do a photocopy, place tally marks beside each client's name. At the end of each month, simply total this spreadsheet so you know what the total day to day expenses were for each client.

You can either bill your client with this figure or file this information for future reference when you review your rates.

Even if you decide not to bill your clients for these expenses, it's still wise to track these items because you should have some idea of what your overhead expenses are should you decide to raise your hourly rates at a later date.

Reminder System for Government Remittances

As a reputable bookkeeping company, it's imperative that you ensure your clients' government remittances are always paid on time.

Sometimes clients can make this difficult by not bringing in their forms or checks, but it's important that you have a system in place to cover yourself and to make sure these critical, time-sensitive forms are paid on time.

First of all, don't ever file away any remittance forms that your clients bring to you. Peg them to a bulletin board so they are always in plain sight. Review them daily.

If you can, have your clients change the mailing address on the remittances so they come right to you. This makes it easier because you will have the form in front of you pegged to your bulletin board to remind you.

Set up a monthly spreadsheet that has a column for each company along with the type of remittance due. In the last column update the status of each remittance (i.e. "called for check," "complete," "picking up.")

Also, make sure you always diarize all remittances in your Day-Timer.

TIP: See the "Government Remittance" form located at **www.startbookkeepingbusiness.net/book-resources/**

Pre-signed Checks

When it comes to making sure your clients' remittances are paid on time, having pre-signed checks is a great option.

Some clients won't mind giving you pre-signed checks. Each check is made payable to the government authority, with the amount sections left blank.

Many clients tend to avoid this because it makes them uncomfortable leaving these checks with you. It may take some time to build up trust with your clients so they'll feel comfortable enough doing this. When you think they'll be open to this idea, try to get them to agree to pre-signed checks because this really can make your job easier. Then, each month all you have to do is fill in the amounts to have the remittance ready to go in seconds.

If you do have pre-signed checks, make sure that you have a good security system in place to store them. Keep the checks in a locked file cabinet or a safe.

Year-end Procedures

Getting your client's financial information ready for his or her accountant should not be a major undertaking if you have kept the information in the client's binder up to date all year long. This isn't always possible as some clients only bring in their accounting information quarterly, semi-annually, or annually.

However, after you have completed each month of the fiscal accounting year, you still should only have the following year-end steps to complete:

1. Set up all Accounts Payables due (but not paid) at year-end:

   - Vendors

   - Workers Compensation Board

   - Government Remittances

2. Photocopy the last month of all government remittance statements.

3. Reverse any old, stale-dated outstanding checks from the bank reconciliation that are more than six months old.

4. Gather all bank statements and canceled checks together.

5. Follow the "Checklist for Client's Year-end" (see Binder Client Sheets for this).

6. Do any adjusting journal entries (cash clearing, etc.)

7. Make a final backup onto CD to put into the front of the binder.

8. Create a new client binder for the next year with new dividers.

9. Transfer final Bank Reconciliation, Chart of Accounts, and Trial Balance at year-end to the new binder.

10. Remove Client Binder Sheets from the old binder and place in the new binder.

Posting Adjusting Journal Entries

When you receive your client's adjusting journal entries from their accountant, here's how they should be posted:

- Post to the first day in the new fiscal year so the entries are easily found.

- Use "YE JE #1" (i.e. Year End Journal Entry #1) etc. as a source code to match the accountant's adjusting entry numbers.

- Any revenue and expense transactions should be posted to "Retained Earnings," *not* to the revenue or expense accounts (you are posting into the current year and you don't want to affect these accounts for the current year.)

Chapter 6: Tips for Running Your Business

In the business world, the rearview mirror is always clearer than the windshield.

<u>Warren Buffett</u>

Tips & Tricks

Recurring Transactions

Use "Recurring Transactions" (Simply Accounting) as much as possible for items such as bank charges, loan payments, deposits, etc. Even if some items have different amounts each month (but use the same accounts), you can still store it as a "Recurring Transaction" and change the amounts as you're posting.

Use Excel

If there are a lot of checks on your Check Register/General Ledger listing (when doing your bank reconciliation), an easy way to find them quickly is to "export" the listing to Excel. Do a "sort" and place your listing in numerical order going from the lowest figure to the highest. This can save you an enormous amount of unnecessary time hunting for the right check amounts.

Cash Clearing

As you're posting your client's transactions, you may come across a deposit or check that you're unsure where to post. Temporarily post this transaction into your "Cash Clearing" account so you can still balance your bank reconciliation. Write the transaction down on a note so you can ask your client about it later. You can also file this note into the yellow "Current" file folder for easy retrieval later.

Don't Call Too Often

Save your inquiry phone calls for when you have thoroughly reviewed all transactions for the month as you may have a list of questions to ask them. Clients get annoyed when you phone them too often with every little question.

Keep Backup Printouts

Attach a printout of your General Ledger listing to the back of all government remittances. Then if you need to go back at a later date to check your figures you can see where you got the figures from. Because we sometimes need to back-post into a previous month, this will throw off our General Ledger listing, making it difficult to find out where the original figures came from. If you have your original printout attached to the remittance, it makes it much easier.

Monthly Bookkeeping

Bookkeeping for smaller clients is much simpler than for larger companies.

These companies usually handle their own bill payments and deposits. So all you have to do is post these transactions every month by tying them into the bank statement. Depending on the size of the books, the total time you spend on smaller clients is generally under four hours.

Here's the breakdown on how to do monthly bookkeeping for smaller clients:

1. Sort out your client's paperwork into the following piles:

    - Bank statements & canceled checks

    - Vendor invoices (accounts payable)

    - Debit and other small receipts

    - Payroll for employees

    - Customer invoices/receipts (accounts receivable)

    - Credit card statements and receipts

    - Government remittances

2. Start with vendor invoices and post these along with the accompanying canceled check that was used to pay it. Enter the actual check number in the accounting system along with the invoice number and amount. Use the date of the check.

3. Post the debit receipts on purchases made through the company bank statement. Any business receipts that were paid out of pocket by the owner are credited to the Owners/Shareholders account.

4. Post any payroll checks that were paid to employees. These are generally done manually (whether you provide

deduction information or the client calculates these themselves). Use any canceled check numbers that you have. I usually will post the full month of payroll even if I don't have all the cancelled check numbers. This is so I'll have all the payroll entries in place to calculate the government payroll remittance.

5. Post any customer invoices as a receivable as necessary. Post any deposits for invoices that were paid by check. You may have to set up a spreadsheet if you have a retail client in order to post daily cash deposits into various revenue accounts. Alternatively, you could enter each daily cash deposit into the accounting program directly. I find using spreadsheets quicker and thus only have one entry to make for this in the accounting program.

6. Finish the bank reconciliation. If you have used the bank statement as your guide for posting, you should balance easily. I find the bank reconciliation in my accounting software works very quickly and easily rather than a manual calculation.

7. Post any credit card payments. How you set this up will depend on whether the credit card is personal or business. If it's personal, run it through the Owner/Shareholder account. If it's all for business expenses, you can set it up as a Credit Card Payable.

8. Do any government remittances as necessary. Watch for deadline dates and make sure you get the information back to your client in time for payment. I like to put a Post-it note with the due date on any filled-out remittances as a reminder for the client.

9. Print off the financial statements, bank reconciliation, and journal entries for your client's binder in their binder. I usually print off two copies of the financials and give one to the client immediately while filing the other.

Those are the steps to do a small company's monthly bookkeeping. You'll develop your own style and method but this is the basic outline for monthly bookkeeping.

Doing Your Own Bookkeeping

You may find after doing bookkeeping day in and day out for your clients, doing your own bookkeeping is the last thing in the world that you want to do.

However, you do have to make sure that you schedule time in your calendar each month to make sure that you stay on top of your own bookkeeping.

You are running a business, after all, so make sure that you give it as much priority as you give to your clients' bookkeeping.

There is no excuse for you, as a bookkeeper, to be behind on your government remittances or to not know how much money you made in the last month. You need to be able to react accordingly if you find that your expenses are exceeding your revenues.

Taking a Vacation

You'll find as a freelance bookkeeper that taking a vacation is not as easy as it was when you were employed. Even though you have the freedom to set your own hours, working with a lot of clients can make finding time to take off a real challenge.

This is especially true if you are offering payroll services for your clients. Most small businesses that require payroll services pay their employees by the hour at least twice a month. This makes taking two weeks off in a row extremely challenging for you as the bookkeeper.

Here are some options that you can use to make this work:

- If you can, arrange to do payroll just before you leave and just after your return (so that you still have two full weeks.)

- See if the client can calculate payroll while you are away (some do this on their own anyway.)

- See if your client is willing to pay their employees an "advance" during this time that you will reconcile on the following pay period.

- Only take one week's vacation at a time.

One of the downsides to being a bookkeeper (whether it's as an employee or as a freelancer) is that the work is always there waiting for you until you return – nobody else does it for you.

So you work twice as hard to make sure that you're caught up on all your work before you go on holidays and then have to work just as hard to get caught up again when you return. The paperwork just keeps coming in.

Nevertheless, you will probably find the best time to take your vacation is during the holiday season as many businesses are closed during the two-week period around Christmas and New Year's Day.

Virtual Bookkeeping

Virtual bookkeeping can be done a few different ways. Some bookkeepers log in to their clients' computers directly from their own and access clients' accounting software that way. Other bookkeepers prefer to do the bookkeeping on their own computer and store the data there.

Either way, your client will have to send you the actual paperwork so that you can process and enter it in the accounting system. Clients can email, fax, courier, or mail this information to you.

Even though many times you won't be meeting your clients in person, you will still need to speak to them on the phone when necessary. For that reason many virtual bookkeepers find that online communication services such as Skype are invaluable in being able to talk to their clients worldwide without incurring huge phone bills.

Helping Struggling Clients

You'll find as you do freelance bookkeeping that some businesses are struggling to survive. You know the ones that are struggling because you see their account balances every month when you reconcile their bank statements.

But there is a way you can help these struggling clients, assuming you have good computer skills. If you have experience putting together basic websites and setting up autoresponders, you could be helping out these clients.

Most small offline businesses have no clue about how to set up their own websites or permission-based email marketing. When they think about typical advertising, they think of newspaper or radio ads, which are extremely costly.

But if your client's cash flow is suffering, they may have to cut their traditional advertising costs just to stay afloat. So what can you, their bookkeeper, do to help them out?

Offer to set up a simple website for them. If you know basic HTML, then set up a static website with a few pages of basic information about the business. If you know how to use WordPress, you can create a website even faster along with adding some great features that WordPress plug-ins can provide.

Then, if you have experience with autoresponders, this is a "must have" add-on service for your client. All businesses can benefit from having their customers sign up for their mailing lists so that they can send them specials offers and keep them informed about their businesses. This helps to build strong relationships with their customers.

The outlay to set this up is minimal compared to traditional advertising costs. The customer just has to pay for a domain name, web hosting, and the autoresponder itself. The monthly cost is under $40, which is a bargain in the offline advertising market.

You benefit from adding this service to your bookkeeping business in several ways:

1.   You get to keep your existing bookkeeping client, which ensures a continued income well into the future for you.

2.   You generate lots of goodwill from your client and possibly even referrals for new clients.

3.   You attract new clients by adding these offline services to your bookkeeping arsenal while charging good rates for this at the same time.

It's win-win for you both. Plus, I can guarantee if you offer to set this up for a client whose business is suffering, they will jump at the chance and be extremely grateful. I've personally done this with great results.

I suggest that you set this up for your existing bookkeeping clients for little to no additional charges. Your goal is to keep your bookkeeping client and help them out at the same time, not gouge them.

Alternatively, you could barter with them if they have something of interest to you. Be creative. You could provide free hosting on your server in exchange for something. I'm currently doing this and it is working out great.

As a freelance bookkeeper, you have the inside information on your client's financial health. It's up to you whether you want to help them out or watch them go out of business.

Conclusion

I hope this book has shown you the steps you need to take to start your bookkeeping business. It may seem overwhelming at first. But if you take each step, one day at a time, and put each procedure that I've laid out for you into place, you'll find that very soon you'll have a thriving freelance bookkeeping business that you are proud to call your own.

I wish you much success in your bookkeeping business.

Chapter 7: Getting Help

All people want is someone to listen.

Hugh Elliott

Sub-Contracting

You may find that after you've been running your business for a while, you have too many clients for one person to handle.

Your choices then are:

1. To turn new clients away
2. To refer them to another freelance bookkeeper
3. To sub-contract the work out to another freelance bookkeeper

Obviously, you'll only make money with option #3. However, there are pros and cons of sub-contracting out bookkeeping.

Pros:

- You still make money.
- You get to keep a new client.
- Your business can expand and grow.

Cons:

- You are still responsible for accuracy.
- Your business reputation is on the line.
- You must find a competent bookkeeper and train him or her to do the books the way you do.

Finding a freelance bookkeeper to help you should be relatively easy. Look for new bookkeeping businesses who have just applied for business licenses. You can also use Craigslist to either place an ad or contact freelance bookkeepers who have placed an ad there.

If you do decide to sub-contract some of your bookkeeping to another freelance bookkeeper, make sure that you create a good contract that spells out exactly what is expected of each of you.

External Advisors

Working at home can be isolating, so having someone to bounce ideas off of can really help. Sometimes you can come across issues that you have no idea how to handle. At times like this, it's very useful to have someone that you can call.

An advisor can be another freelance bookkeeper, an accountant, or even another home business owner.

This is where networking at local business events can really pay off. Don't make the mistake of only looking for potential clients when you attend these events. Yes, the freelance bookkeepers that you meet are your competition, but they also may be a source of referrals and assistance if you need help.

Simply Accounting Training

There are many places to get training for learning Simply Accounting. However, start with the Simply Accounting support page for the best training tips.

http://www.SimplyAccounting.com/SupportTraining/

QuickBooks Training

QuickBooks offers classes and services to help you learn this software.

http://QuickBooks.Intuit.com/Product/Training/QuickBooks-Training-Solutions.jsp

Peachtree Training

Peachtree offer training for their software including guides and software.

http://www.Peachtree.com/SupportTraining/GetTraining/

Bookkeeping Associations

As mentioned in the section on certification, joining a bookkeeping association can be very beneficial to your business. Not only can you network with other freelance bookkeepers but they can also help you find clients if you are a registered member.

Canada:

The Institute of Professional Bookkeepers of Canada (IPBC) – www.ipbc.ca

United States:

The American Institute of Professional Bookkeepers (AIPB) – www.aipb.org

Australia:

The Australian Association of Professional Bookkeepers (AAPB) – www.aapb.org.au

United Kingdom:

The Institute of Certified Bookkeepers (ICB) – www.bookkeepers.org.uk/

Real Life Accounting

This is a twenty hour online course that requires no textbook or live instructor. It is a self-paced tutorial that can be taken conveniently in your own home or office. It's for bookkeepers (or non-bookkeepers) who need to brush up on bookkeeping basics.

The topics covered are:

Phase I – Accounting Environment

Phase II – Accounting Principles

Phase III – Accounting Elements

Phase IV – Accounting Tools

Phase V – Accounting Practice Example

Phase VI – Accounting Analysis

If you preview the first section (which is FREE), the course instructor, John Day, will send you a two-volume valuable resource called *Accounting Solutions for Small Business: A Compendium*. This resource is full of tips from Day's "The Journal Entry" newsletter.

http://www.RealLifeAccounting.com

Bookkeeping Websites

www.StartBookkeepingBusiness.net

This is my website where you'll find a lot of articles and additional information on starting a bookkeeping business.

As mentioned throughout the book, the following resources…

- Sample bookkeeping business plan
- Spreadsheets to track client information
- Client forms
- Marketing materials, etc.

…can be found here:

www.StartBookkeepingBusiness.net/book-resources/

Get Bookkeeping Clients

This is my bookkeeping promotions website where you'll find tons of sales letters and other marketing materials to promote your bookkeeping business.

www.GetBookkeepingClients.com

The Freelance Bookkeeper Blog

My friend Gabrielle Fontaine runs this blog and posts first-rate articles on freelance bookkeeping.

www.TheFreelanceBookkeeper.com/blog

Starting a Bookkeeping Business Books

"How to Start a Successful Home-Based Freelance Bookkeeping and Tax Preparation Business" by C. Pinheiro, EA & Gabrielle Fontaine, CB

"Start & Run a Bookkeeping Business" by Angie Mohr, CA, CMA

Chapter 8: Interviews with Freelance Bookkeepers

Genius is one percent inspiration,
ninety-nine percent perspiration.
Thomas A. Edison (1847 - 1931),
Harper's Monthly, 1932

Interview with Nicole Fontaine
www.PrecisionAccounts.com

Nicole Fontaine of Precision Accounts Bookkeeping graduated from Sprott Shaw in Kamloops, BC in 2005 with a Diploma in the Legal/Admin Assistant course.

In October 2008 she opened the doors to pursue self-employment with Precision Accounts.

Nicole has worked in the Administrative field for approximately 5 years in both Alberta and British Columbia. Prior to her new business venture she took some time to upgrade her skills to better prepare herself and her confidence for the world of freelance bookkeeping.

What made you decide to start your own bookkeeping business?

Once I found out I was pregnant I lost my job and racked my brain thinking of options for stay at home moms. After a conversation with my sister-in-law, the idea of bookkeeping was brought to my attention and I fell in love with the idea and began taking courses for the next year to upgrade my knowledge and prepare for my own business.

Where did you find your first client and how long did it take to find them?

I actually found my first client before I opened for business. To test the waters I placed a free classified ad on a local website and they responded within about 2 weeks of the ads run date. They are still a client and one of the best ones!

How did you transition into your bookkeeping business? (i.e. did you work full time and do bookkeeping on the side part-time?)

I have a very supportive spouse who has been here for me the entire time. When I started my business I had an 8 month old baby and was collecting EI (Employment Insurance) so I had some income coming in which helped.

What were the biggest challenges you faced when you first started out and how did you manage to overcome them?

My biggest challenge was overcoming the fear of starting my own business. I never thought I was ready, my self confidence was really lacking, so after spending thousands of dollars in education, the savings account ran dry and I figured it was either now or never.

When I got my first client I had a wave of relief when I realized it wasn't as scary as I had thought it was going to be. I was used to working for large corporations and this had left me wary of what I was getting into, but I soon realized that small businesses aren't on that same spectrum.

My next issue was my age as most people expected someone older to show up at their business, not a woman in her early twenties! I created a set of "Sample Books" to show my potential clients I knew what I was doing.

I still deal with this challenge but have been able to collect testimonials from clients. Basically it all comes down to first impressions.

What advice would you give to a bookkeeper wanting to start their own bookkeeping business?

Stay focused, you will meet many challenges along the way but as with all things in life you will overcome the obstacles. It won't come overnight, but if you stay focused on the end result you wish to obtain, you will make it.

I recommend creating a business plan, it will help you along the way to stay on track and realize where you want to end up.

What sort of training and experience did you have before starting your business?

I took a Legal/Administrative Assistant course from a community college and had worked in head offices and large corporations in both BC and in Alberta doing Administrative work (Payables, Receivables, Payroll, and everything else that was thrown my way from the Controllers and the Presidents) so I had basically experienced all areas.

While I was pregnant and after the birth of my daughter, I took about 10 different courses though different colleges, spent my savings and realized I had re-learned everything ten times!

How do you promote your bookkeeping business? What types of marketing has worked well and what has not?

I have used sales letters which had about a 5% success rate, as well as free classified ads, correspondence with other bookkeepers, newspaper ads and so on.

I would say the best way has been word-of-mouth through my clients, family, and friends. I am working with more accountants this year, so I am hoping to expand through them as well.

My worst return on investment was the newspaper.

What other services do you offer your clients besides bookkeeping?

I offer T1 Tax preparation for my clients.

What mistakes did you make when you were first starting out and how did you overcome them?

My one mistake was accepting each and every client who called. I learned very quickly that there is such thing as a "bad client". I wasn't getting paid on time or I just wasn't getting paid at all.

Now I have implemented a retainer fee and a service contract which outlines all terms.

Do you have a bookkeeping website and if so, how did you go about setting it up?

Yes I do, I decided to create a one once I got familiar with how the World Wide Web worked.

Do you have any tips or techniques that help you efficiently manage your bookkeeping business?

Never file away remittances, even if they are not due for a month. Always keep them in sight, refer to them and write them in a day planner, whatever works. When you are dealing with multiple businesses it's easy to forget about them, especially if it's a small client you only see once every few months.

Also, let your accounting software work to your advantage, they have implemented transaction storing for a reason so use all these features to their potential to help save you time.

What steps do you take to ensure that your clients always pay your invoice on time?

I use a retainer fee. If they are good clients, I bill monthly and never have an issue. If they are "unorganized" with their bills, I continue to request retainer fees once the last one is used.

Do you have an "External Advisor" (i.e. someone you can contact) if you have questions about your bookkeeping business? If so, where did you find them and how have they helped you?

I have a family friend who has been doing books for many years and she has helped me when those "strange" things come up that were not covered in my 10 courses! No matter how many courses you have taken, real life scenarios are never covered in a text book!

As well she helped me to organize my needs for starting a business, letting me know what I could get away with not having initially and what things I should make a larger investment in. I also have a CGA (Certified General Accountant) in the family so that can be wonderful at times.

Interview with Michelle D. Savoy
www.SavoyBookkeepingAndTax.com

Michelle Savoy is the President of Savoy Bookkeeping and Tax Services, a company specializing in accounting, bookkeeping, payroll, tax, and training services. She is a QuickBooks Instructor at Mesa Community College, Phoenix Community College and a partner with Maricopa Community College Small Business Development Center. She is a highly rated professional known for her ability to communicate complex accounting and tax matters in an easy to understand practical manner.

Michelle has over 20 years of experience and advance training in accounting and taxation. She received her formal education from Chabot College while pursuing her Accounting degree, The American Institute of Professional Bookkeepers, The National Association of Certified Public Bookkeepers, The National Association of Tax Professionals, and she is currently pursuing the Internal Revenue Service Enrolled Agent certification.

She is a former employee of Associated Third Party Administrators, the largest third-party Union benefit administrator and processor in the nation, KPMG Peat Marwick LLP, then one of the six largest CPA Firms in the world, and the Oakland Athletics Professional Baseball Company, a Major League Baseball team. In her capacity, she supervised an accounting department with a staff of seven, managed multiple client's books and financial records, and reported directly to the Chief Financial Officer and Board of Trustees.

Michelle continues to be of service to the community and small businesses, helping them improve their financial opportunities and keeping their businesses growing in the right path. Her expertise and knowledge of taxation and accounting will continue for years to come.

What made you decide to start your own bookkeeping business?

I wanted to spend more time with my family.

Where did you find your first client and how long did it take to find them?

My first client was a referral from my Accounting Manager at the time. My Manager connected me with a woman that ran a consulting service and she needed a bookkeeper to service several of her clients. Within my first year of opening an office I had ten bookkeeping clients.

How did you transition into your bookkeeping business? (i.e. did you work full time and do bookkeeping on the side part-time?)

I started freelance work while working full-time. I later found a part-time job that would cover my monthly expenses and allow me to have more time to build my practice.

What were the biggest challenges you faced when you first started out and how did you manage to overcome them?

My biggest challenge was learning how much to charge for my services. In the beginning I did quite a bit of Pro Bono work because clients would always express financial hardships but I soon realized that I was merely taking on their problems by working for free. I also realized that people have a choice on how to allocate their finances and I found that oftentimes people would splurge on things that had a far less value than the services I was providing.

What advice would you give to a bookkeeper wanting to start their own bookkeeping business?

I would recommend setting up their administrative and client policies and procedures first. It saves a considerable amount of time when a system is in place to service clients.

What sort of training and experience did you have before starting your business?

I had taken college-level accounting courses plus 10 years of bookkeeping experience.

Were you certified by a bookkeeping association and if so, how has it helped you with your business?

No, I am not certified but I have completed all of the certification training. I do plan to take the exam this year.

How do you promote your bookkeeping business? What types of marketing has worked well and what has not?

I work with the Small Business Development Center teaching QuickBooks courses at the local Colleges, which has increased my client base. I receive referrals from current clients often. As for what doesn't work, I have had only one response from the numerous direct mail campaigns.

What other services do you offer your clients besides bookkeeping?

I offer payroll, tax preparation, tax representation, and training.

What mistakes did you make when you were first starting out and how did you overcome them?

My most notable mistake that I am still working on today is not implementing a system that streamlines my processes. Accounting services seem to work best with a system and some uniformity to avoid duplicating your efforts. I am working on perfecting a system that works seamlessly from marketing to providing a service.

Do you have a bookkeeping website and if so, how did you go about setting it up?

Yes. CPA Site Solutions is the absolute best website provider for the accounting industry.

Do you have any tips or techniques that help you efficiently manage your bookkeeping business?

I recommend implementing a system for your service processes to avoid spending non-billable time on repetitive tasks.

One of the changes I recently made is I defined the difference between bookkeeping and write-up services so I now bill more for bookkeeping (which is the detail work) and less for write-up work (which is the summarization and review of my clients recordkeeping system.)

Write-up work is a great revenue generator for me because in the past I only marketed my outsource bookkeeping rather than reviewing and producing financial statements.

What steps do you take to ensure that your clients always pay your invoice on time?

I set all clients up on recurring payment and I require a retainer equal to the first three months fee or $300 minimum, whichever is less. The retainer is used for office consultations, telephone communications, email, mail, faxes and one-month of service if needed.

Do you have an "External Advisor" (i.e. someone you can contact) if you have questions about your bookkeeping business? If so, where did you find them and how have they helped you?

I have two advisors I call almost daily and I have two other advisors that I call occasionally. I met all of my advisors at continuing education training seminars.

Appendix

Step By Step Plan

Here is a five week step by step plan to help you get started:

Week 1:

1. Set up your office
2. Get all licenses and permits
3. Name your business
4. Research pricing

Week 2:

1. Complete business plan
2. Decide on sources of revenue

Week 3:

1. Set up client systems
2. Create file systems
3. Set up computer systems
4. Establish backup systems
5. Write engagement letter & services form if using
6. Create client intake form

Week 4:

1. Set up advertising budget
2. Develop logo
3. Type sales letter
4. Create a mailing list

Week 5:

1. Contact accountants for referrals
2. Prepare "elevator speech"
3. Investigate business groups to join
4. Place an ad on Craigslist.org.

INDEX